contentment

rebellion

assimilation

USA

Papaya Head

The Life
Cycles
of a First
Generation
Daughter

By **J. Nwando Olayiwola**, MD, MPH, CPE, FAAFP

Dear President Napolitano:
Thank you for creating a
UC where voices like mine
can be heard. Enjoy the
book!
                    Love,
                        Nwando

To my parents, Prof. (Dr.) Okey L. Onyejekwe and
Prof. (Dr.) Egondu R. Onyejekwe, to whom I owe it all,
and to my husband Paul and our children,
Darius Olaoluwa Arinzechukwu and
Nissi Oluwapamilerin Amarachi,
to whom I give it all.

*This book is dedicated to the many
First-Generation and Second-Generation children
who walk a number of fine lines, sometimes scared
to fall on either side, and sometimes finding it hard to
strike the right balance. In the end, trust me,
those falls and imbalances will bear fruit.*

Overview

As a physician, I am accustomed to specializing in medical training based on age/stage of the patient – e.g. Neonatology, Pediatrics, Adolescent Medicine, Internal Medicine, or Geriatrics, and thinking of patient issues by system – e.g. Cardiology, Neurology, Psychiatry, Nephrology, different surgical subspecialties, and more. With all of these options in front of me, why did I then pick Family Medicine, which, depending on how you see it, is agnostic to age/stage and encompassing of multiple specialties? While the purpose of this book is not to discuss my career selection, there are many parallels to the life and experience I have had as a first-generation daughter in America and the fact that I became the kind of doctor that I am.

From my experience and those of many I know, the typical first-generation child, born of immigrant parents, goes through three life cycles: assimilation, rebellion and contentment. These are not necessarily in sequence, not necessarily in isolation, and not necessarily the same length. It is possible for the child to assimilate and rebel at the same time; to become more content and assimilate at the same time. None is superior or inferior. However, attaining that phase when contentment dominates the rest is one of the most beautiful and gratifying experiences we ever have.

Enjoy this colorful journey as we walk through the life cycle of a first-generation daughter. I hope you will laugh, cry, but most important…understand.

Contents

Life Cycle 3: The Contentment

"Whenever you wake up is your morning"

— Igbo Proverb

LIFE CYCLE 1
The Assimilation

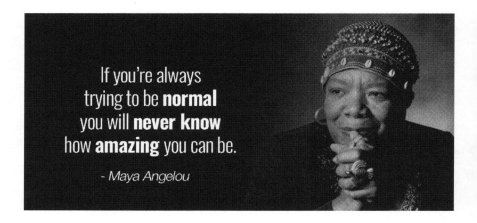

If you're always trying to be **normal** you will **never know** how **amazing** you can be.

- *Maya Angelou*

At this stage all we want is to fit in, to look the same, be treated the same and not stand out. As assimilators, we are full of self-doubt, shame, embarrassment and uncertainty. Our "normal" is not the "normal" of the world around us, and we wrestle with the question: "is anything normal at all?"

CHAPTER 1

Nigerian Soukous

One of my earliest memories as a child is in the first house that my parents were able to get for us, a rented house in a nice quiet court in Columbus, OH, in what was and still is an all-white, all American part of the city. In their minds, they were on the verge of the American dream – my father having completed his PhD from the Ohio State University, my mother her Master's degree from The Ohio State University. They were full of optimism, leaving the rented off campus student housing where they and their first three children lived, making a new life for their fourth child who would be born in this house on That court, and creating a space for the litany of relatives (true and extended) that would soon come and call Columbus home. I remember the pride on their faces as they showed us the four bedrooms and the 3 bathrooms, the backyard, the basement- space for us kids, at the time ages 6, 5, and 4, to play and be free. We would no longer have to live the hushed-up life of being crowded in a 2-bedroom apartment with neighbors who were predominately student families, shushing us for being too loud, with nowhere to play except the makeshift park we invented in our minds in the concrete parking lot.

My parents believed that if they worked hard, they could go from renting such palatial real estate to owning it. They worked hard, encouraged us to work hard, and started to build their own "normal" on That Court. Slowly, uncles and aunts started coming from Nigeria to stay with us. We were so excited as kids to have these older but not old relatives who we could talk to, learn from, and who served as babysitter for us during the many days and nights our parents were hustling to feed the ever-growing family. They were also there to make sure we did our house chores, completed our homework, and abided by the rules of the house in the absence of our parents.

Given that our parents were some of the earliest Nigerians to live in Columbus, OH, our family, and our home, was a gateway for many of the subsequent Nigerians who came to Columbus for school, work, or a better life. At any given moment in my life, there were "uncles" or "aunties," a salutation we were taught to bestow upon any Nigerian or African who was older than us, that came to live with us. Some stayed for one month, some stayed for years. Some were blood relatives, some were related by the common thread of their status in America –foreigners seeking all that this land of opportunity could offer us, and while most were Nigerians, many were not. In fact, the complexities of Nigerian ethnic divisions and African country lines were unknown to me until I went to college. We listened to happy and hearty music, sung by Nigerian Afrobeat and highlife musicians such as Fela, Rex Lawson, and Osadebe; soukous music; Brazilian music;

Ghanaian musicians such as the Ramblers and African Brothers Band; reggae, soca, salsa, calypso…we listened to it all.

I knew my parents were Igbo and that my father spoke 2 of the major Nigerian languages, Igbo and Yoruba, fluently. I knew that they spoke Igbo to some of their friends and that they spoke pidgin English to others. I knew that they tried to speak broken French to others. I knew that they were from Onitsha and Owerri-Nkworji in two parts of Southeast Nigeria. I knew there was a big map of Africa with over 30 countries in our living room. But I thought that Bob Marley and the Wailers were from Nigeria, that the African Brothers band was Nigerian, and that soukous music was Nigerian. Everything fit neatly into that box. In fact, crossing that threshold with black skin, a thick African accent, and that 1970s butterfly collar gave these uncles and aunts immediate access to my box, immediate crowning as uncle or aunt, and immediate respect and good manners from me and my then two, and later three siblings.

It was not until I went to college and got in an argument with a fellow Nigerian student, who scoffed when I told her that a soukous band was Nigerian, that I realized any difference. I was playing a cassette tape of my father's and we were planning a dance for African night at the Hale Black Cultural Center at The Ohio State University. She publicly embarrassed me and said that this was a Congolese band and that this was squarely Congolese music. I was shocked. In fact, I called my parents that night and said, "Daddy, did you know that soukous music is

Congolese?" expecting him to be as stunned as I was. He laughed and said, "yes, of course."

"How come you never told us that?" I asked.

"Would it have mattered?" he asked, in that loving and sagely way he always handled those teaching moments. "What would it have changed?" And at that moment I realized that he was right. I loved my box. I loved feeling this connection to people who were different like my parents, different like me, and it would not have mattered to me then, when that quest for normalcy was such an important part of my life. It was much later in my life that I found out that this uncle was from Warri in Nigeria and was not Igbo, this Aunty was from Benin Republic, that Uncle was from Ghana, those Uncles were Yoruba, that family was from Delta State. In Nigeria, some of these people would rarely talk to or trust each other – here, they shared a bond that made those divisions seem so trivial – they needed each other to survive.

Chapter 2

The Party Goes On

Everyone came to our parties. My parents were known for throwing good parties. We would hear this United Nations of uncles, aunties and families talk all of the time about their struggles at school – "ol boy, they no fit pass me in dis class. Professor talk say he no dey understand me." They talked of their struggles at work – "which promotion? Abeg, promotion go pass me again." When my mother finished years of study and an incredible thesis for her PhD in zoology, and she went before the panel to defend her research work, she went hopeful, believing that she had accomplished a major feat with three kids and one on the way. Uncles and aunties advised her on what to wear, how to temper her accent, how to be normal, not to sound smarter than the professors, and other advice.

In the meantime, the party plans for her PhD celebration were underway. We couldn't wait. There would be food, drink, music and happiness. We kids didn't really know what it meant, but we had gone to our father's PhD graduation a few years before, so it made perfect sense that our mother would have the same one. When our mother came home from the committee meeting and told us that she was denied her PhD, she was in tears. She said that one of the panelists spent more time asking her about her children – how many she had, how many she was expecting to have, how old they were, who stayed with them at home – and many other questions that would be illegal today, but were not in the 1970s. After completing years of doctoral work, in the end, they actually told her: "as a black foreign woman with two kids and one on the way, we don't feel that you are ready for this. You can't do both." They actually said that. And that was it. Fail. Done. Period. With fire in her eyes, when we got older, she told my siblings and I: "do not ever let anyone stop you. Not because of the color of your skin, your name, where you come from…" and she looked at my sister and I…." or because you are a woman. They may have closed that door on me, but I know God will open another one." My brother and I were crying about the denial of this PhD, not knowing exactly what it was or what it would have changed, but because someone had told our mother that she could not get something because of us. As we grew up, we promised each other, in our own childlike way, that we would never be an obstacle to our parents again. We would be good kids. We would listen to the rules. We would clean our rooms. We would not argue with each other. We would finish our food. We would help take care of our younger siblings. We would take care of our parents. Later when we were in middle school and our mother finally received her PhD, we felt an unusual source of pride because of OUR role in helping her get there. And there was no greater lesson that a parent could give their children on perseverance. That PhD was a collective win for us all. Since then, I have believed I can do anything that I want, no matter what.

The party went on. A few people cried with my mom on the first day. By the weekend at the party, no one was crying. Everyone was jovial, celebrating as if she had received two PhDs, eating, dancing, laughing, living. She was so determined to move on and fight the good fight that people could not help but join her in that conviction. Her faith inspired the many other African women who used to come to our house. Her story was the story of so many African women immigrants in that time. Many were fueled by this challenge, others gave up, some changed courses. But in our little community, regardless of what happened "out there," my parents created a safe place for this village to grow and be.

Chapter 3

Papaya Head

I thought it was perfectly normal when my mom's two younger brothers, who now lived with us, would come home to our house on That Court with a live goat, and tie it to the long steel beam in the basement. My older brother, my younger sister and I loved to go to the basement and look at the goats when they came. We would sit and wonder what the goat would taste like in the stew, the okra soup, the egusi soup, the ngwo-ngwo (goat meat pepper soup). Would this goat be hard or chewy? Would its skin have that burnt taste we liked? Sometimes we would throw them grass to eat, and sometimes we would taunt them. Sometimes we would name them. By the time they were on our dinner table in our food, we either liked or hated the goat, and the goat probably liked or hated us.

During our taunting, with me always the furthest away because of my fear of animals, but making the loudest noise, we had confidence that our uncles tied the rope securely around that steel beam. Until the day we maybe taunted a bit too much and one angry goat, who we called "Sheep," broke free and chased us through the house. It was incredibly scary, having an angry goat, who knew he had nothing to lose because he would be dinner soon, chasing three screaming kids throughout the house. We ran all the way from the basement to our parent's room on the top floor of the house and slammed the door shut, until our uncles came and re-captured Sheep. After that, we stopped taunting goats for good.

One day, when our father had traveled, our uncles were out of the house, and the three of us were home with our mom, we heard loud yelling on our front porch. We went outside to find our mother yelling from our porch at our neighbor, a very angry white man who used to call the police when we had parties, only for the police to say we were not disturbing the peace. He was heaping loads of incredible insults on our mother, using words we had never heard or words we had heard but could never say. That was the first time we had ever heard the word "Nigger." Each of us remembers this experience vividly, as it birthed many questions and challenges for us.

"Go back to Africa you stupid nigger bitch!" he said, his eyes full of rage.

"Leave me alone, you papaya head," our mother responded. We all looked at each other: "Papaya head?" His insult seemed way worse than papaya head!

"Get out of our neighborhood and take your fucking monkey family with you."

"Shut up, you coconut nose!" she screamed back.

"What kind of fucking name is that?! You mean the coconuts that you monkeys and your monkey children swing from trees to get?"

My brother had had enough. "Shut up, leave our mom alone." My sister and I were speechless. He had just said "shut up," to an ADULT, in broad daylight, in front of our mother. But, my mother didn't scold him or stop him. In fact, she looked at him lovingly.

So when he said, "shut your nigger goat flesh eating mouth up boy," to my brother, my sister and I felt it was game on. "You shut up." "Don't talk to us like that." "Mind your own business." "Leave us alone."

"Go back to the jungle you came from and have your litter of babies there! That's all you guys know how to do, have babies!" he screamed. My eyes briefly met his little daughter's eyes. She was about the same age as my younger sister and she looked frozen in disbelief.

"If you keep harassing me, I will call the police, mango eyes!" my mother shouted back. Our mother firmly intended on using every tropical fruit she could find to insult this man, so we joined the program, taking turns heaping the fruitiest lashings at this man, enjoying the colorful salad we were creating. "Banana neck!" "Grapefruit eyes!" "Tomato ears!" "Pineapple teeth!" "Plantain arms!" Each fruit made him angrier until my mother finally took us all inside. Like clockwork, the three of us wanted one more shot at this man and we all said, as we entered the door, in our loudest voices, "papaya head!" one more time.

When we went inside our mother hugged us all and told us she was sorry that we saw that. We found out that he had done this a few times before and that she had shielded us from it. She told us she was proud of us for standing up for ourselves and that we should never let anyone talk down to us like that again. We were so distraught, as this was our first time experiencing something like this. She had the exasperated look of someone who had been through this before. We wanted to talk more about it, but when my brother asked, "Mommy, what is a nigger?" She said, "You guys go to your rooms and don't ever tell an adult to shut up again."

But we could not get over the "Papaya Head" incident, as it notoriously became known. Why did that man hate us and our mom so much? Why did he call us monkeys? Why did he make fun of us eating goats? What was nigger? Were we from a jungle? Why did he hate us so much? What did we do? It was a very troubling experience for three children.

It was at this point we started to question our "normal" life. We did stand out a bit. No one else had parties in *That* Court. No one else we knew from school or the neighborhood had so many languages spoken in the house. No one else we knew had and killed live goats in their basement. No one's parents talked like ours did. Maybe that was why our mother didn't get the PhD. These questions beat at our juvenile minds like rain on corrugate rooftops. There were no answers, only questions.

Later we heard our mother talking her two brothers out of going next door and beating up the man. She insisted that they would go to jail and no one would ever take their side, no matter what we said. When our father came back, he filed a formal harassment complaint against our neighbor for the torment he inflicted upon our mother repeatedly. We had no idea that the "Papaya Head" would deliberately wait until all of the men left the house and he could catch my mom on the porch or in the backyard to start his tirade. She endured it and endured it until her children saw it. I don't know what ever became of that complaint. All I know is that my siblings and I would always walk close to each other when going out in *That* Court, and were fearful that the "Papaya Head" would snatch and chop us up if he ever got close to us.

Chapter 4

What's in a Name?

After the "Papaya Head" incident, nothing seemed normal. We did not want to seem different anymore, so that no one would humiliate our mother like that again. We started believing we were different and that we had to fit in. We became conscious of our parents' accents. We did not want them to speak Igbo to us. Over the next few years, my sister and I no longer wanted the "African" hairstyles, such as threading, that our mother used to do for us. We wanted to be normal, and in our minds, normal meant white, American, long silky hair, speaking English, not having thick accents, having names people could pronounce. Normal. The same. Not different.

My parents, in the meantime, were going in the opposite direction. When they had the first three kids, they were adamant that we should all have proper English or European first names, so that we would fit in and blend with others. They gave us Igbo middle names, which was what they called us at home. However, by the time our baby brother came, they took pride in the beautiful Nigerian names we had, and they gave him two Nigerian names, no English name. They were evolving, maybe rebelling, maybe just content with who they were.

However, the name issue really created a difficult dichotomy for us. My older brother was named Lawrence Okechukwu Onyejekwe, Jr., after my father, who went by Okey (the short form of Okechukwu). As many Nigerians did in those days and still do, we called my older brother "Junior" at home. I smile as I think that we actually still call him that now. His name was relatively easy – he was named after his father, which was very important at that time. Somewhere in the early years he was called "Larry," not by us and not by our parents, and that stuck with him for many, many years. My sister was named Sylvia Ifeyinwa Onyejekwe, and we have always called her Ify, which is the short form of Ifeyinwa. Ify was her name at home and somehow, again I am not sure how it happened, Sylvia was her name at school. Sylvia was an English name my parents adored, and they felt it was very befitting. Our younger brother, who was born when we lived in *That* Court, just a few months before we moved to McBane Street, was named Chukwuemeka Nnamdi Onyejekwe, and is, and has always been called Emeka (short form of Chukwuemeka). I am always jealous at how he was spared the anguish of a name identity crisis.

However, my name experience is more dramatic and traumatic. I was born as Jacqueline Nwando Onyejekwe. My parents chose Jacqueline because of Jacqueline Kennedy Onassis, whom they admired a great deal. I too came to marvel at "Jackie O" later in life. I had developed a great sense of pride in my name, Nwando (with the "Nw" pronounced was if the "N" is silent). I was named after my paternal grandmother, Nwando

Omameh Onyejekwe, who died when my father was 7 years old. By all accounts from my parents and my uncles, my Grandmother Nwando was a beautiful and courageous woman. Our name means "the child will be a shade for the family," and my parents always told me that I was special, the glue of the family, the one who would care for all of us. I loved the name, and I loved my Grandmother whom I had never met. I used to imagine what she would look like and picture her telling me to take care of my siblings, to be a good girl, to be a good student. I adored her. In Kindergarten, my teacher, "Mrs. A" as we called her, loved the name too. Although my official name was always Jacqueline Nwando, she was happy to call me Nwando. On the first day of school she said: "I see you have two names. What do your parents call you at home?" I said: "Nwando." She said "Nwando it is," and took time to make sure she said it right, and the classroom said it right. It was so validating… "what do your parents call you at home?" That simple question gave me dignity and the opportunity to be the same person at home and school.

I was not so lucky in the first grade. Although I started off trying to be called Nwando, in the second week of school we had a substitute teacher, a young, vibrant white woman who the class thought was so much fun. As she went through the roster, I could see the ceremonious pause that all teachers seemed to have as they got near any of our names. Then – "Jacqueline….Nawanda…N-wand-doh….On..yi..juke..wee." The whole class laughed. I spoke up and said "Nwando."

"What about the rest of it?" she said.

"Nwando Onyejekwe," I said.

"Then what's Jacqueline?" she asked.

"It's my other name but I go by Nwando," I responded.

"No..wand..dough?" she attempted again.

"Nwando," I said, becoming more and more embarrassed.

"Why is the 'N' there if you don't say it?" she asked.

"Because 'Nw' is one letter in my language," I replied.

"How can two letters be one letter? What kind of language is that?" she joked, and the class was wild with laughter. "Does that make any sense to you?"

"No," I said. "It doesn't. But it's true."

"Well this is taking too long, and that name is too hard. We are going to call you Jackie. Class, call her Jackie," she said.

"But," I tried to say more but was already crying.

"That's that. Jackie it is. I'm not even going to try your last name. We could just do Jackie O. honestly."

I couldn't object. I was surprised at how quickly all of my classmates, who had walked in that morning calling me Nwando, so comfortably started calling me Jackie. Not even Jacqueline. But Jackie. And in that singular moment, one that I will never forget, I started straddling the lines of a name at home and a name at school, an identity at home and an identity at school and I can say that my journey to reclaim my name identity started as soon as I lost it.

I know so many kids like me, First-Generation children of immigrants, who straddle those lines every day. In some ways, it's a blessing to be a different person in different arenas. In the years the followed, "Jackie" was the person that everyone saw outside, but "Nwando" was the one that everyone knew at home. No matter what "Jackie" faced at school – all of the girls ignoring her for 6 months in 4th grade, being called an "African booty-scratcher" in 3rd grade, getting made fun of for her hairstyles, being teased for her parents accents when they came to school – "Nwando" was always her Grandmother's namesake and a light in her family at home.

Chapter 5

The Weight of the World

Being black in America, being an African in America, being an immigrant in America, you subconsciously assume the identity and the fight of every person that looks, sounds, smells or shares anything with you that's different than the mainstream. And, unfortunately, as a kid, that is too much weight to carry on your shoulders.

Being in class for many years as the only black person was tough for my siblings and I in school. Though our parents moved us from the public schools that we attended when we moved to McBane Street, a few miles away from *That* Court, to St. Andrew Catholic School in Upper Arlington for better educational opportunity, those years were and still remain heavy on us all. We went from being one of a number of black kids in the school and in our classes, standing out more because of our names and our Nigerian heritage than our color, to being the only black, African or any kind of minority in our classes in the Catholic school. My parents believed that this was emblematic of their progress – being able to put their kids in a costly private school in a wealthier part of Columbus. And kudos to them for doing what they did. However, we really struggled with our identity as a result.

In class, when a teacher mentioned Africa, the entire class would look at us, as if we must be able to finish the sentence. We all dreaded when the textbook had its customary short chapter on the slave trade or callout box on Martin Luther King, Jr. Every time these things would come up, my siblings and I could feel ourselves shrinking inside, hoping that, for one moment, no one would notice we were black.

The whole "not noticing" wish is one that many of my friends who are people of color can relate to. Slowly, over time, whether it is from blatant attacks by the Papaya Head type or silent subtleties by the media, in which we rarely saw ourselves depicted positively, you start to believe that the skin you are in is the inferior skin, and that somehow you missed out on the right color. You start to think your life would be that much easier, so much more wholesome and fun, if you could have only been white. But, maybe if you talk like them, walk like them, eat like them, think like them, play sports with them, attempt to do your hair like them…no one will notice you are black. Brilliant! They won't even realize! If you start to accept this name, "Jackie," which sounds more like their names, maybe you will fit in. I started telling my siblings and other family members to use the name "Jackie." It would be so much better for me if I did that. My parents and many of my aunts and uncles refused, but many also conceded and this experiment in being that other person ensued.

By 7th grade, the transformation was complete. My sister and I got single braids with extensions and went from wearing our own hair as it was to braiding it, because it made our hair longer. When we first went to our respective schools with these braids, having left our natural hair out for bangs so it wouldn't look too unnatural (unbelievable!), the attention was unprecedented. "Wow, your hair grew that much?!" "how did your hair grow that fast?" "is that your hair?" "can I touch it?" It was unbelievable, that power of hair. The curiosity and confusion of our white classmates, teachers, principals, school parents, neighbors, and everyone around us was actually quite comical. We had come up with the perfect retort – "I used *Miracle Gro* and it worked!" We'd joke later at home at how stupid some of their questions were and how little they knew about people who were not like them. Meanwhile, we knew so much about them. It was a great period of short lived triumph – we were now involved in conversations about hair with the other girls – silly, trivial conversations that only white girls could have – did you use Pantene, how do you crimp it and get it to stay, should I perm it, should I straighten it, it's so hard to manage, but what will I do with it in the summer, I think I want bangs, I washed it this morning and it took forever to dry, I need a new conditioner that gives it more body...But we joined in now. And when they asked, "do you wash your hair every day?" we would respond, knowing that we did not and could not, "of course, that's gross not to!"

And I was really happy with how much they seemed not to notice that I was black anymore. I was one of them, accepted, similar, no different. Until one day a group of my Pantene-speaking "friends" came to me and said they had an idea that I was going to love. They suggested that I date the only other black kid in our grade, and that we would make a cute couple. Never mind that he was much shorter than me, totally socially awkward, wore glasses too big for his face, stunk in sports and had a baby voice – he was PERFECT! When I asked the girls why they thought I should date him, not even mentioning that I was not allowed to date, one spoke up and said, "because you're both black." And there you had it – transformation failed. They still noticed.

Chapter 6

Black Coffee and Oreo Cookies

Everyone noticed I was still black. The white people noticed. The black people noticed. As much as I tried to assume the likeness of my white classmates, it was still noticeable. My skin would crawl when I heard the word "black" used in any context, hoping it wouldn't be a derogatory reference to my family or me. But, in many cases, it *was* a reference to me. Even mentioning the word "black" made people think of me.

One morning, in ninth grade, the girls in my class were excitedly talking about how they had started drinking coffee and were going to drink coffee as we entered into final exam season. They went on and on about how many flavors there were to choose from and the different options for enhancing the taste. I listened and laughed, knowing I would never be allowed to drink coffee at my age, but always intrigued by these lives the other kids lived and the ease with which they moved from topic to topic as if they owned the world. Then one said, "I don't like anything in my coffee, I prefer it black." They all paused and looked at me, then looked at her in disbelief that she had uttered the word in front of me. "Sorry Jackie," she said. "I can't believe I said that." I could not understand the apology.

"Why are you sorry?" I asked.

To which she replied: "I didn't mean to say, you know, that word, you know. I didn't mean to offend you."

"How does talking about drinking coffee black offend me? What does that have to do with me?"

She squirmed a bit and the others also became a bit more uncomfortable. "Well, because you're black."

I had no energy anymore – here I was, trying to disappear from being black in my behavior, attitude, thinking, dressing, talking. But in their minds, I was emblematic of not just all black people, but EVERYTHING black, even coffee. The situation disturbed me immensely. I started to realize that I did not just represent all things black in their eyes, but all things non-white. For my white friends at school, I would not be much more than this, no matter how hard I tried.

But I still tried. For some reason, I felt that I could still go down this path. My sister and I took a liking to the rock and roll bands of the late 80s and early 90s- Skid Row, Poison, Bon Jovi, Queensryche, Red Hot Chili Peppers, INXS, Motley Crue, Guns N Roses and more. Much to our parents' annoyance, we became bigger fans of these groups than our white friends, with posters on our walls, attempts to copy their hair and styles, and full-blown adolescent fan behavior. Interestingly, we were also completely smitten with R&B singers like Jodeci, Keith Sweat, Prince, Michael Jackson, Janet Jackson, Jodi Watts, New Edition, En Vogue, Troop, Hi-Five and others. We knew the words to all of their songs, listened to them at night in our bedroom, tried to sing and dance like them. We even used our stereo system with cassette recorder to make mix tapes. When one of the songs we liked came on the radio, we would rush to the stereo and press "record and play" to record the song on our mixtapes. However, that was life at home, not at school.

One day, in 9th grade, one of the older black girls at my very private school came up to me and said she wanted to chat with me. She and I had played basketball together and she was a big fan of mine, as I was a 9th grader playing varsity basketball as point guard who changed the entire experience of basketball for the school. What she told me shocked me. "We notice that you don't hang with any of the black people at school. Some of the black people are calling you an 'oreo cookie' and I wanted you to know that."

"What does that mean?" I asked innocently.

"It means you are black on the outside and white on the inside," she replied. "That you act like a white girl. Like you're ashamed of being black."

I was speechless and immediately defensive. "So, because I don't hang with the black people at school, I am an oreo cookie and ashamed of being black? I *am* black – I listen to black music; my whole family is black. How am I not acting black?"

"The fact that you just said that...." She started. "Girl, don't be mad at me. I'm just telling you what is being said because I like you. I don't want people making fun of you." And she meant it. She truly did care about me – I didn't really know it then, but she helped me a lot.

I was totally confused...how would I resolve this dilemma? My life was full of so many contrasts. For example, the kids at school would rush home to watch their favorite TV family, the Huxtables, a black family, an all-black and proud family, but would not give us the time of day at school. They would dance to "Bust a Move" by Young MC and sing all of the words, even try to talk like him at the school dances...but no one would dance with the black girl at the dance.

One day, I went to dinner at my friend's house after school. She was from a well-established family, her father a professional, her mother a stay at home mom, which was the case for many of my classmates' parents. As I struggled to make sense of the meal of cheese covered cauliflower, which they were all eating with me, I thought a lot about what my family was eating.... probably Nigerian jolloffe rice and stewed meat. My thoughts were interrupted when my friend's mother turned to me and said: "We like you Jackie. You're not like other black people. You are always welcome here." Now, in her mind, she meant that as a compliment, but when I went home that night and discussed it with my parents, my father almost went to their house to reprimand them. He told me that this was "the biggest insult of your life." That I should never feel proud of someone making such a comment, because it is less of a compliment to me than it is an insult to the entire race. Cheese-covered cauliflower met oreo cookies. Everything was heavy. Too heavy for an adolescent kid.

Chapter 7

All in the Family

In second grade, we had a class project in which we were asked to draw our families. What a blast for a kid! Who doesn't love drawing their family at that age? I remember taking special care to draw all of my family members, in the right proportions, and with accessories that singled them out. I was so proud, and I turned it in to the teacher. A few minutes later, as the teacher looked through them, she called me back up to her desk.

"You are supposed to draw your family," she said.

"Yes, I did," I responded.

"You drew…" and she started to count the people in my picture. "You drew 13 people."

"Yes, I did," I said.

"You are only supposed to draw your family," she replied.

"That *is* my family," I stated, completely confused about the issue.

"No, it is supposed to be your actual family, the people that live with you," she responded, impatiently.

"That is my family. Those are the people that live with me," I responded.

"You cannot possibly have 13 people living with you. Do you have a mansion?"

"No."

"And all of these people actually live with you?"

"Yes."

"And sleep at your house and wake up there every day?"

"Yes."

She was totally flabbergasted. She then stated: "Well these are not all your family members the way we mean family. Your family is your parents and your brothers and sisters. Next time, only draw them and not all of these other people!" She handed me the drawing back and I still did not understand. How could my uncles, aunts and cousins not be family? Who defined family anyway?

Meanwhile, in first grade down the hall, my younger sister was having a similar conversation with her teacher about our family size, unbeknownst to me until my brother, sister and I were walking home from school.

We usually got home before our Uncle, our mom's youngest brother, who would be coming from the high school about 15 minutes after us. When we got home that day, we met a nice white man and woman, who were waiting for us on the front porch. They asked us if our parents were home and we said no. They asked if they could talk to us, because they wanted to take us to a place that would be so much fun for kids. They then told us about this fun location they wanted to take us to, and that our teachers at school thought it would be a good idea for us to go. At this place, we could play pool, go swimming, play games all day, meet cool kids, amazing adults, and have the time of our lives. They asked us if we wanted to go to this fun place and we could meet other families that would make sure we had nonstop fun. We were excited as we heard more, and we unanimously thought, "sign us up!" We had no idea that this was Children's Services and that they were plotting with our teachers to take us from our parents. As we went upstairs to get our swimming clothes and a few other clothes, our Uncle came home, chatted briefly with the people and kicked them out of the house. He was so angry – we had never seen him that mad! "Do you guys know who those people were and where they wanted to take you?"

"No," we said in unison.

"They were like children's police and they wanted to take you away from us, away from me. They were going to take you to go live with other families, probably split you up from each other, and never let you see your Mommy and Daddy or any of us again."

We were stunned! He told us that the teachers at school were "concerned" that we were living in an unsuitable environment, full of too many people and without appropriate attention and love. We were in tears. Who loved us more than our family, our parents, our uncles and aunts? How could we have ever lived without each other and our baby brother? Why would someone want to steal kids away from a loving home? Our teachers had it wrong. Our environment was similar to homes of many immigrant families – full of uncles, aunts, cousins and others – sometimes related by blood but most often related by situation and origin – and always full of love. My uncle couldn't sleep for days after this episode, nor could my parents. They warned us to never let people in the house again and to NEVER agree to go anywhere with anyone no matter what they promised. They told us that we were special and could not have lived without us. As I think back on my family portrait, it could not have been more familial.

Chapter 8

Subtle Papaya Heads

I never realized how many more Papaya Heads we would face in our lives. Sometimes, it was blatant. One year, we finally convinced our parents to buy Christmas lights, so we could mount them on the house. This was one of those things that First-Gen kids often had to explain to their parents and nag them incessantly to do. My parents could not understand why something like this was so important. Why would people spend their money, buy lights and mount them on their house for a few weeks? Lights that served no purpose except to fit in. Lights that were not biblical. They were too busy thinking about their jobs, their security, our school fees, their families back in Nigeria, their friends struggling in America, and their constant fight to exist and be equal – there was not enough time for Christmas lights. As we drove through our neighborhood every year during Christmas season, we noticed that one dark house. Our parents didn't know it, but those lights were not just about Christmas for us. The lights were about fitting in. The lights would be a way to not *always* stand out. We were always different, no matter how much we tried to fit in. The absence of lights was a reminder that the family in that house was not the same as the others. So, we begged, and nagged, and one year, our mother finally agreed!

We were so excited! We went to Kmart to look for lights and didn't even know what to buy. We ended up choosing multi-colored lights that we could hang from the lower roof and were so excited to put them up. My older brother and Uncle hung them up and the rest of us stood by and watched, filled with the eagerness that one only has when they feel a life change coming. As we plugged the lights in and watched their glow fill what was once a dark space, I could feel myself gasping – we were in, we would fit in, we would be the same.

For the next week, my sister, brothers and I could not wait until dusk, so we could plug the lights in and flip the switch on. Our parents still did not get it, but they let us revel in this new feeling of normal. Until one day, we came home from school and as we had become accustomed to doing, we looked at the lights. We were shocked at what we saw – the cord to the Christmas lights had been cut, severed smoothly with scissors, and on the exterior wall near the outlet where the lights were plugged, in black spray paint read the following: "leave niggers." No one could speak. That evening, our lights no longer shone, literally and figuratively, and as my Uncle painted over those words, we all silently decided that we would never ask our parents for such frivolous things again. A house full of Christmas lights would never change that we were an immigrant, black, African family that just did not fit in.

But sometimes, papaya head behavior was much subtler. My siblings and I do not have enough fingers to count how many times we heard – "sorry I am not allowed to play with you," "my mom said I can't play with you guys," or "I'm not allowed to come to your house." Or when we played outdoor games with the neighborhood kids and a Mom called her kids into dinner, then they turned to another kid playing with us- "do you want to come over for dinner?" – this was a question we were almost never asked. Or my personal favorite – one of the girls in my sixth-grade class was having an end of the year pool party at her house and invited the entire class, in which I was the only black person. The whole class was gearing up for weeks. Two days before the party and the last day of school she came to me, flanked by two other girls in the class, and said: "Jackie, I'm sorry, you can't come to my party anymore. My mom said we don't have enough plates." To which I said: "Don't worry, I won't eat." She looked at her two moral supporters and then back at me. "Well, we don't have enough cups," and she looked over at her supporters. I got it. I shrugged and said "Okay it doesn't matter. I don't even want to go," then I left and went to the bus. When we got home, I told my siblings through tears what had happened. My sister said: "I'm just glad you didn't cry at school. Her party is going to be boring anyway."

Sometimes, we didn't even realize the disparagement that was occurring. Very frequently, the neighborhood game of the evening was "Cowboys and Indians," in which the fearless, heroic cowboys would always defeat the pathetic, troublesome Indians. It was years before we realized how awful and derogatory this game was to Native Americans, and before we ever questioned why we were always the Indians. Here is how it would go – one of the kids would say, "let's play Cowboys and Indians," and me or one of my siblings would invariably say, "Ooh...I want to be a cowboy!" "Sorry," the kids would say, "you guys have to be Indians." We'd play in this horrible narrative, not understanding the actual narrative, running around acting wild and crazy until the cowboy shot us or tamed us. Finally, years after we had played this game outside with the kids in the neighborhood, always the loser, the wild one being tamed, the player being shot, my younger brother excitedly told my father how he did a double spin move to escape the cowboy, proud of his agility. My father said, "Wait, what was the name of that game?" And we told him. "And what is the point of that game?" And we told him. He looked bewildered. "And you were an Indian?" And we told him we always were. "Never, ever play that game again. That is an insult to Native Americans everywhere. And never play any game where you are always the loser. If you play that enough, then you will believe that nonsense." None of us ever played that game again, and as we got older and understood the non-glorified textbook version of the atrocities committed against Native Americans, we were surprised that anyone ever would.

Chapter 9

Girls Things, Boys Things

I think one of the evolutions of the first-generation child is being able to see, understand and appreciate the evolution of their parents over time. A couple of years ago, I sent my father pictures of my daughter, his first granddaughter, at age 4, in her soccer uniform, on her first soccer team. "She looks adorable," he said. "I'm glad you are starting her young!"

What a contrast to his beliefs a few decades ago when I was in seventh grade. I had just transferred to a new, posh, private school in Columbus, as a 7th grade girl, already nervous about if I would fit in or not. While my previous school had volleyball and cheerleading for girls fall sports, this new school had soccer. We kids had all realized, not necessarily at the same time, not just that we were each awesome athletes, but that one of the keys to success and acceptance in a Midwestern American town was being a star athlete. This was your key to the after-school talk, camaraderie, weekend inclusion in events, and if you were lucky, actual friendships.

By this time, I had already excelled as a softball, basketball and track athlete, and really wanted to start my new school, in the first sports season, playing soccer. The soccer coach saw me running in gym class during capture the flag, he immediately started recruiting me and felt that with some coaching, I would make a fine soccer player. My brother was already playing soccer and had made waves at the school. I was so excited. We were definitely a soccer family – we rallied around the TV and watched the World Cup every four years, saw the kids playing soccer with makeshift balls in their bare feet back in Nigeria and loved to join them, and shared the excitement with parents as our Uncle (our Mom's youngest brother) was recruited from the local high school to play soccer at The Ohio State University! We were definitely a soccer family.

So, I assumed it would be easy to just ask my parents to register me for soccer at school. The look of disbelief on my Dad's face when I asked is still ingrained in my memory. "No, absolutely not," he stated. "Girls don't' play soccer."

I tried to argue with him. "Yes, they do, Daddy. They have a whole team of girls that play soccer at Wellington."

"How can girls play soccer? Soccer is not for girls where we come from. They don't even have a World Cup for women," he replied.

"But the Coach thinks I will be good at it," I responded. "A lot of girls are good at it."

"You are NOT playing soccer," he concluded. And that was it. The tone let me know that this case was closed, at least at the moment.

I was shocked and sad, but very soon started to advocate for my situation. I went from *wanting* to play soccer to believing that I *needed* to play soccer and be good at soccer, if for nothing else but to change my Dad's mind. I started what most kids in my situation would do. I began a grassroots advocacy campaign to change the conversation. All of my siblings, my Mom, and our Uncle were recruited to this campaign and our mission was simple – change Daddy's mind and convince him to let Nwando play soccer – using whatever vantage point you have with Daddy. Everyone was on board with this plan, and everyone had a role to play. Here is what our campaign looked like for two weeks, all of us realized that our father would need to come to the decision on his own and not feel forced into it or mutinied against– I gave everyone their charges:

Mommy's role as a strong advocate for women's rights and someone who constantly broke glass ceilings for women in Nigeria and in the U.S.: subtly infuse comments about how angry you and Daddy were in Nigeria when you and other women were not allowed to join the sports teams at University of Nigeria, Nsukka. Remind him of how happy you both were to fight and win that battle before, and how you hope your two daughters don't have to keep fighting for their rights to be on an equal field with boys.

Uncle's role as an active soccer player at a major university and the person who would train me privately to shine in this sport: show Daddy pictures and tell him stories about the college women's soccer team, how much you realized that women were excelling at the sport, and that you would personally take the time to make sure I was well trained.

Older brother's role as the child that my parents tended to listen to first, who often brought a balanced perspective to the most heated conversations and was also at the same school as I: convince Daddy that this experience is essential for my wholesome growth at the school, and that participating in soccer would not harm my grades, but in fact enhance them. Let him know that you would personally make sure I was completing my academic work on time and adequately preparing for my examinations.

Younger sister's role as the child that won the "it's not fair" award in our summer recreation program when she was in third grade, then and now a staunch fighter for equality, parity and justice: gently point out the contrasts in Daddy's thinking about this – he didn't want me to be a cheerleader at the previous school last fall because it was "too girly and provocative" and it was not a sport in his eyes. If they have a team at the school, it is because girls can actually play soccer. And if that failed, remind him of the double standard- that our older brother could play and Nwando couldn't.

Younger brother's role as the cute last child whom everyone adored, but also the increasingly threatening and locally famous soccer star whom the family invested a lot of money and time in, from a young age, on soccer: in your own cute way, let Daddy know that you think it's only fair that I am allowed to play soccer and if I am not good at it, I'll stop. Ask him what he is afraid of. Sometimes when people have to explain things to children, they realize some of the contradictions and issues with their platform.

My role: continue to watch all of the sports I watched with my father, demonstrate my love for sports in general, and especially soccer if we were watching it. And sit back and let my advocacy army work for me.

After a few weeks of this pressure, from all angles, my father acquiesced and said that I could indeed sign up for the soccer team! It was a great victory, and one of many such victories that we achieved for girls in our house.

The soccer story was an interesting contradiction in itself. From a young age, and definitely drummed into our heads repeatedly during high school and college, our father impressed it upon my sister and I to work hard, study hard, and achieve our goals so that we could be independent of any man. We have wonderful memories of these conversations – "put yourself in a position where you don't have to rely on your husband or any man for anything." "Don't be a woman that depends on any man." "Be a strong and determined woman." "Don't let any man hold you back." "Believe you can do anything a man can do, and even better." "Be excellent. Always go above and beyond." These were the kinds of charges he gave us and we accepted, as we navigated the complex labyrinth of boundaries and intersections in our lives.

My father did not attend my soccer games when I was at The Wellington School for 7th and 8th grade, or as a 9th grader on varsity. He was always proud to hear that I was the leading scorer in all of those seasons, MVP for girl's soccer, and being recruited by other high schools to play for them. It wasn't until 10th grade, when I transferred to Bishop Watterson High School, a much stronger school athletically and especially in soccer, that he became interested. I went from being the varsity MVP as a 9th grader at Wellington to a junior varsity 10th grade player at Watterson. He was confused and started to come and watch.

The first time he saw me play he said: "Wow, you are very, very good. These girls are very good. But why didn't they put you on varsity?" My father has always been like that – he wants us to excel at everything and wants everyone to see that excellence in us. He was angered that the soccer coach didn't see that in me, even though he had not seen me play until then. From that day forward, he was committed to making sure I "moved up." He had my younger brother and uncle, the soccer stars, work with me and help me develop more finesse with the ball, did drills with me to improve my agility and stamina, and spent even more time watching soccer games with me and pointing out skills I could work on. By the end of the 10th grade season, I was moved up to Varsity, and in 11th grade, was a starting right forward. My father and mother attended every game they could as their schedules and the schedules of all of my siblings permitted. My father's investment in my soccer career made me more motivated than ever.

About a decade later, my father's younger cousin, who used to live with us and was now raising his own family, was in a similar situation. His daughter, my younger cousin who has always been my little protégé, wanted to play soccer. And though the times had changed, my cousin was in the same battle I had been – her father did not want her to play and didn't believe girls should play soccer. Fortunately for her, my father was like a big brother to hers, and he often took my father's advice on matters of raising children. The day we heard our father telling our uncle to let her play soccer without a fight, that girls can be very good at soccer and it would be enjoyable for him to watch her play, my whole army smiled at each other. And I have forever respected my father for embracing the change that came with being an immigrant and the changing of times.

Chapter 10

I Was Born Here

As I mentioned, the first part of our life cycle as first-generation (First-Gen) kids, children of immigrants, was assimilation. All we wanted to do was fit in, be the same as everyone, and be "normal," whatever that may be. My siblings and I, though in this phase at different times and different lengths, shared this common experience of trying so hard to create this identity that wasn't ours, and that could never be ours. In fact, we were so often told that we were not American, because our parents were immigrants, that we would introduce ourselves and forcefully remind people that we were born in America.

An example would be in a classroom or on a team when the teacher or coach would make the infamous pause the first time they saw our last name. We always knew when they arrived at 'Onyejekwe' because of the facial contortions, dead silence and glaring at the roster to figure out how to pronounce it. "ON-YA-JOCK-WUH, is that right?" When we were younger and embarrassed of everything that called attention to our differences, we would agree, "yes that's right." Our father later told us to make people pronounce our name right, and to correct them if they were wrong. "They will pronounce Eastern European names with multiple consonants back to back, so they

43

can pronounce African and Indian names if you correct them," he always said. In this life cycle, however, we were not ready for that. So, when the struggling roster reader said, "where is ON-YA-JOCK-WUH from?" we would say: "It's Nigerian but I was born here." And every time I would say it, I would hope that the conversation would end there, and they would move on to the "P" last names. But sometimes, I'd get that one that wanted to push my buttons… "It doesn't matter, your parents are Nigerian, so you're Nigerian."

Our rejection of the Igbo language can be partly blamed on this quest to assimilate. In the 70s, when we were young, our parents tried to hold on to their culture by speaking Igbo to us. This is the story of almost every Igbo family I know in America whose kids, for the most part, don't speak Igbo unless they came from Nigeria when they were older and had already learned. Our childhood Pediatrician advised our parents to immediately stop speaking Igbo to us, and that we would be very confused and slow if we were learning two languages at the same time. Also, he advised them, it will be easier if we could speak English well – we would get further in America. Couple that bad (and inaccurate, as we know now) advice with kids coming over to our house and making fun of the way our parents and uncles talked, how they spoke and the intonations of our language, and there was no way we would continue to speak Igbo. This is not unique to Igbos but a common story of some of what the first-generation children will shed to fit into their new reality. And for their parents, language is a part of the identity that they mistakenly think can be paused while they get settled and then picked up later.

I cringe now when I think of my siblings and I laughing at our parent's accents with our white "friends" from school, acting like we couldn't understand when they spoke Igbo to us, or pretending as if we didn't understand or support some of the cultural traditions we had. Little did we know, and perhaps the biggest irony of it all, was that this loss was a major loss to us, a part of our identity that would be hard to reclaim, and one that we would beat ourselves up for shedding as we grew into the other life cycles.

No matter how many times we said "…but I was born here," it didn't, nor could it ever erase the fact that:
…. our skin was chocolate brown
…. our parents had thick Nigerian accents
…. our last name was authentically and unequivocally Nigerian
…. we smelled like stockfish and goat meat when we went to school, and we could not cover that smell with all of the perfume in the world
…. we ate eba (fufu) with okra soup with our hands and enjoyed it
…. we had a freezer with isi ewu (goat head) in our basement and we ate it in soup
…. asking our parents if we could have boyfriends or girlfriends would be followed by a threat to send us back to Nigeria for school and have our hair cut low(my sister and me)

.... we enjoyed Nigerian, Ghanaian, Congolese and other music

.... we ate sugar cane straight from the stalk

.... we would always be questioned at Customs when returning from Nigeria upon suspicion that our dried leaves for soups were marijuana or some other drug

.... our hair was kinky and curly

.... we used outdoor latrines and palm leaves for toilet paper when we visited Nigeria

.... we had to translate for our Grandmother when she came to the U.S. – at the doctor's office, with our friends

.... our "family" did not meet conventional, American norms of composition

Therefore, being "born here" was not enough.

LIFE CYCLE 2
The Rebellion

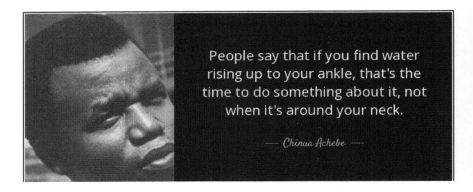

People say that if you find water rising up to your ankle, that's the time to do something about it, not when it's around your neck.

— *Chinua Achebe* —

At this stage, the FirstGen becomes exceptionally jaded by the periods of rejection by the mainstream, self-doubt, and self-hate. We realize that being born here is not enough. We cannot easily assimilate into the dominant culture – they don't want us to and it's not easy to do. So, we become angry, furious, and the pain of realizing that we cannot be part of the mold makes us reject everything about it.

Chapter 11

Niggers and Bathrooms

There is only so much one can take. As the first-generation child tries to assimilate, they continue to run into the Papaya Heads that won't let them, the system that won't let them, the corridors of privilege that won't let them. This is hard for my friends who did not come from immigrant families to understand. I always ask them using sports analogies, "Can you imagine every time you go up to bat in baseball/softball that you start with two strikes, automatically? Or every time you start a football drive you are on the 4th down? Do you realize the kind of pressure that places on that batter up or that drive? Welcome to my world."

I'd say that many experiences continued to shape my thinking how and if I fit into the world around me, and whether or not this world wanted me in it. I was always so proud of my siblings – we were all smart, talented, and had a lot to offer the community in which we were growing up. But this community did not always know it.

Most people think of the bathroom as a sanctuary, a refuge of sorts. When children have an accident on themselves, the parents frantically search for a bathroom to hide and handle the embarrassment. When someone is crying or upset, friends take them to the bathroom to compose and collect themselves. And sometimes, when a black immigrant child needs a place to hide away for a moment at school, the bathroom is perfect. And so it was for my sister and I, in 9th and 11th grade at the same high school. We always looked forward to the opportunities to see each other at school, and when we experienced the many microaggressions, the girls' bathroom was a safe space to just breathe in and out.

One day, my sister sought out that sanctuary in the bathroom at our high school. Normally, I would not have known, as I was already in my first period class, when someone came to the room to get me, saying, "the Principal wants you to come down because your sister is making a scene." I was excused from class and went down to the first floor, only to find my sister outraged and in the face of the Principal in the girls' bathroom. When I asked what happened, she and one of the other five black students in our school, also a family friend who was as irate as my sister, pointed at the black spray paint on two of the bathroom stalls – "NO NIGGERS."

I was stunned at this sight, but more stunned by the Principal who was telling me to calm my sister and the other girl down. "No," I said. "I am not calming them down. What are YOU going to do about this?" He responded, "I already told them that we are going to erase and repaint it, but they won't listen." To which I replied, "yes but what are you going to DO about it? Are you tolerating this in this school? How are you going to get to the bottom of this? What's the plan?" The more we realized he had no plan except to repaint the stalls the more upset we became. As the scene grew bigger, he asked the Vice Principal to take us into the office and speak with us, while he made some calls to erase the words. One week later, the words were still on the stalls, so the bathroom was no longer safe for us. And because the culprits were never found, questioned, or chastised, the school was no longer safe for us. I was halfway through my junior year and very plugged in with outstanding prospects in track and soccer, so I stayed, but my sister transferred from the school the next quarter. And then there were four....

Chapter 12

Reminders, Reminders

Sometimes, our experiences were not blatantly racist or discriminatory and sometimes they were not even intentionally negative. We had to remind ourselves that our parents put us in these wonderful, reputable schools so we could acquire a strong education and be well-rounded as we prepared for collegiate life. That they bet on America as a bastion of hope, equality and safety for their children. That being smart and talented would silence the Papaya Heads in our lives. Being a star athlete in my school helped repress some of the negativity I experienced otherwise. I could run on the track, focused on my sprint races and not think about anything except winning. I could take tests and focus on excelling and not missing any questions. I tried very hard to consume myself with the things that did not make me think about my differences. But, every now and then, as the popular 80's ballad went "there [was] always something there to remind me."

One of the girls who I considered a good friend in school, and still consider a good friend until this day, was always full of questions for me about my life and home. I never took her curiosity as offensive. In fact, I appreciated the fact that she wanted to know so much about me and would also keep it real about what was being said about me. For example, once, as we neared the time for the prom, she asked me if I was going and I told her I wasn't. She asked me why I never go to the school dances and I told her that no one ever asked me to. And she said, "Yeah, I don't think anyone will ever ask a black girl to go." Although inside of me, I kind of thought that already, I was surprised to hear her say it, so matter-of-factly, so innocently. "Yeah, and I don't even want to go with anyone anyway," I responded. But did I? Should I? Did it matter that I consistently missed school events like this? Was it better that I didn't go? Looking back on it now, I know I didn't miss a thing, but as an adolescent trying to understand herself, I reflected on this comment for months.

Chapter 13

The Color of Blood and the Blood of Jesus

This same friend, who I was able to share deep thoughts and experiences with, also used me as a learning tool to better understand people who didn't look like her. She never ceased to amaze me. One morning, in the middle of homeroom, she turned and asked me, "Do black people bleed red blood?" Now, this was not a question I had ever heard, and I really had no reason to wonder about the color of blood. When I first started my periods, I remember my Mom rushing me upstairs, past my Dad, Uncle and brothers cutting their hair in the bathroom, who asked, "What's wrong?" and she replied, "None of your business." I remember talking about blood then and learning of the cultural taboo of discussing this "issue" with the males in my family.

I remember being taught to watch out for the pain that came with t*hat* blood, to be prepared for *that* blood to come at different times each month until it became more regular, to know *that* blood could be extremely heavy and soil my clothes, and to alert my Mom if *that* blood was clumpy instead of thin. I remember feeling awkward around my Dad, my brothers and my uncles because of *that* blood, and scaring my sister with my experiences with *that* blood, letting her know I would help her understand it all when *that* blood came to her. I remember staining my uniform with *that* blood, when it was heavy, and having to stay in the school office multiple times because of it. I also remember *that* blood causing me such pain that I had to be rushed to the emergency room for fear of appendicitis and finding out that the times that I had *that* blood could cause such severe pain. I don't remember, however, ever thinking of a difference between the color of *that* blood and the blood that came with my huge abrasion when I stole second base in softball and cut my knee (I was safe though). And, until that moment, I never, ever wondered if my blood, *that* blood or any other blood, looked different in any other human beings. My entire life, I assumed we all bled the same color of blood. So, I responded, "Yes, we do." But now, my subconscious assumptions about blood were questioned, I followed that yes, with… "Do white people?" And she was surprised. "Of course we do, silly!"

Thankfully, I was raised to believe, both in my two Catholic schools and at home, that we were all sinners saved by the blood of Jesus. Now *this* blood…this blood was powerful, life-changing, purifying, all encompassing, caring, giving, red in color, but color blind. *This* blood didn't cause pain – it freed us from pain, sheltered us from pain. *This* blood didn't stain our clothes – it gave us new garments and a cloak of righteousness. *This* blood washed us as white as snow. *This* blood unified Jews and Gentiles and was the ultimate sacrifice for all of us. I couldn't get enough of *this* wholesome, powerful blood that made us new people and one body in the name of Jesus.

I looked forward to Sunday mornings, where my family would go to church and learn more about *this* precious blood, and some of us would even partake of *this* blood. One Easter Sunday during my first year in college, my friend and I were at home from school and went to church with my family at our old elementary Catholic school parish. How wonderful to hear the priest share his sermon on this incredible sacrifice and the blood of the Lamb, and present to us the Body of Christ, followed by the Blood of Christ, and ask us to partake in both in memory of Him. And then perhaps a child's favorite part of the Catholic mass, "Let us offer one another the sign of Christ's peace," which is the call to break the church silence and shake hands with your neighbors, sharing the love and unifying peace that *this* blood gives us and saying "peace be with you." On this particular Easter Sunday, my little brother reached out to shake the hand of a young man, about 18 or 19 years old, offering him the sign of Christ's peace. He refused to shake my elementary school brother's hand. Then my sister offered her hand and he looked her right in the eyes and shook his head. His father prodded him to extend his hand. It was now a challenge. When my friend, followed by me, extended hands to offer that sign of peace, his father, now red-faced with embarrassment, tried to get him to shake our hands, to which he finally said loudly, "I'm not shaking any nigger hands." We all sat there in disbelief as he went with his father to go partake of the Body and Blood of our Lord Jesus Christ.

Chapter 14

Tropical Friendship

Many immigrant children will relate to the experiences I had in finding close friends in high school and college. Friendship is such a complicated entanglement. Why does anyone become friends with someone else? How do people stay friends? What is true friendship? Is it seasonal? Situational? Opportunistic? Durable?

My best friend in high school ended up being an Indian-American girl, the daughter of South Indian parents who, like mine, came to America to give their children a better life and expected excellence in all they did. We initially came together because of our advanced classes in math and science, but as we studied together, we became intricately connected through our common experiences. We came from countries that were former British colonies. We ate food that was different from our classmates' in texture and spices. We loved academics and learning. We both wanted to be doctors. We came from tropical countries and were used to using bathrooms in holes in the ground and on toilets. We heard other languages spoken in our homes. We had names that our classmates found hard to pronounce. We were scared to death to talk about boys and sex, out of respect for our parents. We liked tea, with milk. Our parents and aunties and uncles had foreign accents. We ate a lot of food with our hands. We were first daughters in our families. We went to Hindu and Igbo or Indian and Nigerian cultural classes and parties on weekends. We had native attire that we liked to wear, and in fact wore for our graduation from high school. We had very high standards for ourselves. We knew what papayas were. We liked mangos.

What a treasure to find and build such an important friendship with a teenager who "got" me! She was Hindu, not Catholic, but went to the school for the education. We studied hard and studied together, relied on each other through awkward teenage years, and as we started to expand our circle beyond the high school in which we were, found out that we were actually pretty, in fact, beautiful...something neither of us knew or thought until 11th grade. We always joked that we brought out the best in each other, possibly including egos. Maybe we literally became beautiful in 11th grade, or maybe it was the confidence and comfort we instilled in each other that brought it out. Because of her, I became increasingly proud of my Nigerian heritage and because of me, she was much more excited about her Indian culture. We would go to each other's cultural events on the weekend, study and eat dinner at each other's houses once a week, learning so much about the other's families, foods and cultures. I learned about Hindu gods and found her mother's shrine at home fascinating, and she learned about why and how Nigerian women use geles to adorn their heads. I missed her when she traveled to India with her family. She missed me when

I traveled to Nigeria with mine. She got me my first sari, though I still don't know how to tie it. My mom made her a simple Ankara dress to wear and she did. We planned to visit India and Nigeria together and started to reject some of the noise we were getting at school.

Through this tropical friendship, we became bold and confident. One day, one of our white classmates told me that another classmate said that my best friend "smells like curry." I knew that I had started to become a different person when I responded – "Tell her she smells like oregano."

Chapter 15

The Boiling Pot

When you are cooking and the pot boils over, sometimes you don't know exactly which ingredient or spice was too much. In this case, it could be the rejection, the humiliation, the microaggressions, the macroaggressions, the obvious, the subtle. It could be the subtext that you're ugly but the realization that you're beautiful. It could be loads of papayas stacked up around you. But, at some point, things build up and it almost feels like a pressure cooker. I don't know exactly the date that I felt this pressure building up, but I know things changed in 11th grade and all of a sudden, I was a very different person for the next few years.

Maybe it was the fact that my uncle and my brothers were victims of racial profiling in high school, college and graduate school. Being out with their friends and experiencing the humiliation of Columbus and Cleveland police questioning why they were where they were, forcing them onto the ground with their hands behind their backs for obeying the law – obeying the written law that is. The more they obeyed the written laws - "don't speed," "don't fight," "don't talk back to police," "don't carry concealed weapons," - the more they were victimized because of the unwritten laws – "don't be a black man in a group of black men," "don't be the only black man in a group of white men," "don't talk," "don't keep silent," "don't know your rights," don't state your rights," "don't move," "don't smile," "don't frown," "don't do anything dumb," "don't be too smart," and, probably the most important.....don't be a black man." One day when we were in high school, my father was driving on the main road to our house, which was in a very nice, mostly white part of Columbus. He was right beside a police officer in the next lane, so he kept a slow pace under the speed limit. After a couple of minutes, the police officer put his alarm on and signaled for him to pull over. The officer proceeded to ask him the following: "Why didn't you want to pass me?" My father responded that he didn't want to speed, and after a ten-minute interrogation, he told my father, "Next time, don't drive so slowly."

I remember my parents having sleepless nights every time my brothers were outside of the house, dreading the call, the call that every black family dreads, that there was a papaya head incident and your son was involved. I remember my sister and I being worried that one day we would lose one of our brothers – either from papaya head actions from the police, or in another unfortunate reality where the papaya heads show up. One of those unwritten rules, not being the only black guy in a group, was one that we had not realized would become so important until later in our high school years. Hanging with their mostly white friends from school, on Friday nights after Friday night lights, at four different times in four different places and on four different occasions, my brothers and two of our male cousins

61

were jumped and beaten by a group of white guys, after being taunted and harassed, called "niggers" and more. In those moments, the group of guys that they were with, in each instance of a papaya head gang-style jumping, none of their "friends" stepped in, tried to stop the attacks, or helped. By the time we found out, it was because a good Samaritan later helped each of them and called their families as well as medical help. Two of them suffered concussions and subsequent disorientation for weeks afterward. This increased the pressure in that pressure cooker that was boiling inside of me.

Chapter 16

Weavers of Nigeria

All the while this pressure cooker was building up, there was another current that was serving as a steam valve, not letting things get too hot. Our mother, realizing that there was a growing Nigerian immigrant community in Columbus and recognizing that this community needed support and encouragement, as well as a way to nurture and organize the children of these families, formed a group called the Weavers of Nigeria a few years before I started high school. The purpose of the Weavers was to "weave" together Nigerian women and their families, instill Nigerian values and culture in their children, and raise kids who were connected, proud of their heritage and part of a larger community no matter where they lived or schooled in Greater Columbus.

Although in 8th grade the Weavers meetings seemed like a burden – we had to clean up the house almost every weekend because the meetings were frequently hosted at our house – I had no idea the kind of blessing it would be to be engaged in this type of community. All of these children, Nigerian children of immigrants or immigrants themselves, were organized and raised by an army of aunties and uncles, who would go to parties together, wear Nigerian clothes, eat Nigerian food, and grow up as "cousins," even until this day. When one of my brothers was jumped by a group of papaya heads, and my sister and I received the call at home, we did not rely on his "friends" that had stood by and watched. Instead, we mobilized our Weavers of Nigeria "cousins," went to the post Friday night football party where he was jumped and went completely off! In that moment, I realized part of what the Weaver's mothers had been doing for us all of those years. While we were all at different schools, with different realities, we were all experiencing common challenges understanding and embracing our many identities. Having these mothers and fathers, aunties and uncles, and older and younger cousins serving as sounding boards and partners, telling each other we were awesome and beautiful, was an important antidote for the other pressures that were building up around us.

This first-generation unity is an indescribable power. We all understand things even without speaking, share jokes and experiences that are hard to articulate. And what is even more beautiful about it is that we share this with other first-generations, regardless of their country of origin. And in many of those countries, we eat papayas for snacks!

Chapter 17

Keeping Eyes on the Prize

The importance of being future-minded and focused in a Papaya Head environment cannot be overstated. It is so easy to succumb to the distractions and mixed signals around you. It's so easy to become consumed or angry by the negative experiences and lose sight of the larger goal. My siblings and I were so fortunate that our parents instilled a very strong sense of learning and intellectual curiosity in us. Our parents did the "clap back" before that was a term. When the guidance counselor in high school told me I was more likely, as a black girl, to get an athletic scholarship than an academic one, as a National Honors Society student and in the top of my class, my parents showed us how to clap back. We were encouraged to keep our eyes on the real prize and end game, our education and our futures.

However, at the same time, we were raised to appreciate the past and present. For years, growing up, our father would have us read articles in *Time* and *Newsweek* to understand what was happening in the world, and also write short synopses interpreting what our young adolescent and prepubescent minds were reading.

As children, we were constantly exposed to some of the horrors that people of color had experienced in the United States, but also in their own countries, so that we could be enlightened about the world but also appreciate what we had. Our parents ensured that we regularly watched programs like Eyes on the Prize, Roots, Shaka Zulu and documentaries on Cesar Chavez, Mahatma Gandhi, Patrice Lumumba, Kwame Nkrumah, Fidel Castro, Che Guevarra, Nnamdi Azikiwe, Nelson Mandela and more. Our father was a professor of higher education at the university, but it was his contribution as a professor of world experiences at home that we all cherish until this day.

One day, in an effort to insult my younger brother, a racist white student with him on the bus, was poking fun at his dark skin, his nose size, his coarse hair. When it seemed that he could not get under my brother's skin with much of what he said, he tried one more dig – "At least my Dad is not a Professor!" At the time, this student's Dad was unemployed, working odd jobs and a few short-term handyman projects here and there. For no reason other than race, he still believed that he and his Dad were still "better than" my brother and my Dad!

The more we watched historical truths and secrets through programs at home and shared these lived experiences, the more blatantly aware we were that the social studies and history we were learning in our schools were half-truths, and in some cases, complete lies. And the pressure kept increasing. How could we be taught about crime in black neighborhoods without having the historical context of segregation, Jim Crow, housing projects, drugs? How could we be okay with millions of black and colored South Africans being separated from the beauties and benefits of their own country under apartheid, while the world watched? I remember constantly being torn between force fitting into a society that didn't value my skin or heritage, to completely extricating myself from it.

Chapter 18

The Pot Runneth Over

A very striking series of events changed my entire outlook on being a young black, Nigerian kid in the United States. In 1988, N.W.A. emerged on the scene with the *Straight Outta Compton* album, which forever changed hip hop in America and the world. NWA took a combination of expressions and realities on race that I was used to hearing from artists like Fela, Bob Marley, and James Brown, and popularized them to tell an urban story that I didn't live myself. However, I admired and respected it because it unleashed a power that I failed to realize that music had. It was, in a sense, a warning cry to all papaya heads – "We can only take so much. We will raise hell. We will express ourselves." Popular culture caught on, and soon we were repping clothes by Cross Colors, FUBU, still without fully realizing the impact of the papaya heads around me. Then, in 1991, at the suggestion of my father, I read the *Autobiography of Malcolm X* and was stunned by the fact that his story had no mention in my history books. And in 1992, when the *Malcolm X* movie came out, it delivered the rebellion that had been growing in me for years. I gave birth to a baby that had waited for its chance. Everything changed. Everything.

I went from trying to blend in with many of the papaya heads around me to the complete opposite, rebelling against anything and everything they did and stood for. I began to take the papaya heads on directly. I'd challenge my high school religion teacher when he discussed the powerful impact of Catholic missionaries on indigenous people in Africa and Asia. I'd ask him to explain more about the atrocities committed against humankind in the name of God and the connections between evangelism, colonialism and corruption. On free dress days at school, my sister and I would wear Cross Colors clothes, Malcolm X hats, black power t-shirts, Public Enemy paraphernalia and Nigerian styles. I started to reject the truth of even being born in America and started saying "I wasn't even born here. I was born there," thinking that would separate me from the papayas.

I became unafraid to share my opinions on issues I used to keep quiet about. I stopped hanging out with white people, stopped going to their events, and sought out a deeper connection to people of color, the places they hung out, the things they struggled with. I was beginning to react to years of being a recipient of hate with delivering a hate of my own. I was quick to get in fights and arguments with people that even looked at me funny.

Now, when people mispronounced my last name incorrectly, as they often would, I took to heart what our father advised us - "Make people say your name correctly. Don't give them a pass.

They can pronounce names that are much harder than yours." I became furious and impatient with people that mispronounced my name. I started to see it as a personal attack, not an accident. A micro-aggression to minimize me and my value. And I would retort, fiercely – "So you can say Schwarzenegger but not Onyejekwe??"

In speaking to so many of my first-generation friends, this is a very common experience. They are so exhausted from trying to fit into the mainstream that they go to the other extreme, so far away from it, and become so hateful of dominant culture, any form of domination and domineering. I became so filled with hate and anger that it consumed me. I spent more time thinking about how I would "clap back" than I spent thinking about how I would personally grow and advance.

In college, my older brother and some of his friends became entrenched in peaceful resistance, learning from many international heroes and revolutionary figures around the world and building a movement that confronted all sorts of "-isms and -schisms". I, too, joined this movement and started to channel my anger at an enemy I did not quite identify, because the more enemies I was angry at, the more enemies I found. It was no longer only the racist, white supremacist papaya heads. There were now oppressive regimes, sweat shop bosses, brutal police, colonial masters, cult leaders, dictators, institutions, drug lords, human traffickers, perps, pimps, phobes, prison-industrial capitalists, segregationists and apartheidists, Jim Crow perpetuators, classists, wars, systems, education – the list was endless.

My pot ran over. My fire was turned to fury. There were so many things that frustrated me. I rebelled against every institution and philosophy that I had been taught. I hated. And hated.

I wanted everyone to pay for my oppression, for my failure to assimilate, for the papaya head hate that was directed towards me and my family for so many years. It was predictable, but not sustainable. There was no way I could continue to live that angry. As Mahatma Gandhi famously said, "An eye for the eye only ends up making the whole world blind." And Michelle Obama said, "When they go low, we go high." My hate was not sustainable.

LIFE CYCLE 3
The Contentment

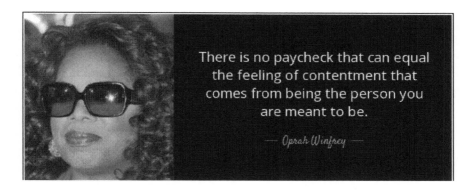

There is no paycheck that can equal the feeling of contentment that comes from being the person you are meant to be.

— Oprah Winfrey —

At this stage, the first-gen reflects more on who they are and who they want to be, the generation that will follow them and enters a stage in which they are comfortable in the skin they are in. There is no need to fully assimilate because we are perfectly content with the backgrounds we have, and the tapestry of cultures and influences that make us who we are. We can infuse components of our identity into the culture around us. We can embrace our roots with pride. We are not ashamed of who we are, because there is a little of everything in who we have become. There is no need to fully rebel in anger because we have channels and strategies to direct our frustrations. We can be vocal without being angry. We reach the stage of contentment and in this contentment, we may not find perfection, but we find peace.

Chapter 19

The Constants

One important way to ensure that the First-Gen ultimately reaches a state of contentment is to have some constant, consistent themes and images in their lives. For me, some of these constants were the emphasis on excellence, particularly in education, and the focus on integrity, honor and citizenship.

In the fall of my senior year of high school, my homeroom teacher was excited for the new class and to better understand each of our personalities and goals.

"I'd like to go around the room and have each of you tell me what you want to do after high school," he said one morning.

I raised my hand – "do you mean which college we want to go to?"

"No, I mean what you want to do after high school. It may or may not be college," he replied.

I was stunned. Literally, until that moment, I thought everyone finished high school and went to college. I had no idea that people did anything else, given my orientation and that strongly instilled Nigerian focus on higher education. As a Nigerian-American child, this was my reality – our parents came to America for the pursuit of higher education, all of their fellow Nigerian and other immigrant friends came to America for the pursuit of education. College was not an option, it was an essential, and, in many cases, one higher education degree would hardly be met with any enthusiasm in a Nigerian-American household. This was a constant, a non-negotiable. So, no matter how hard we tried to assimilate or rebel, my siblings and I always knew that we would be pursuing advanced degrees and higher education.

This theme and value has been the bedrock of the successes that Nigerian immigrant, and many other immigrant families, have seen. It has been essential in my focus since childhood, and interestingly, is something I can now impart to my children.

Chapter 20

Hair Journeys and Views

"Remove the kinks from your mind, not your hair."
Marcus Garvey

"Why does your hair curl up like that?" one of my middle school friends asked me at a swimming pool party. "It was straight and then you got it wet and it just curled up like that."

"How did your hair grow so long that quickly?" another girl asked when I got a full set of long box braids in 8th grade.

"If you don't straighten your hair with that cream stuff, what will it look like?" a fellow high school classmate asked me.

"Not to be rude, but is that a weave?" one of my co-workers asked me.

"Wow, can I touch your hair? I've never seen anything like it," yet another colleague asked me.

"The school does not allow girls to wear their hair in wrap styles. It looks a bit too ethnic," I was advised, at the risk of detention, by one of my high school nuns.

"I would recommend that you don't wear braids or any other unprofessional hairstyles to your medical school interviews. If you can straighten it before you go, I think they will take you more seriously," a college advisor told me.

"Is that your REAL hair? How long is your REAL hair?" my daughter is frequently asked.

"For the recital, all of the girls need to have their hair in a long ponytail with a high poof," we were advised by my daughter's dance teacher.

"Do black women change their hair so much because they have hair problems?" asked another one of my co-workers.

The natural hair movement has been an inspiring movement to watch and be a part of as a black woman. The hair journey for black women often follows the same stages I described for the First-Gen. For me, it started off with trying to have my hair "blend in" with the other girls at school. I thought that maybe if I had it straightened, got a jheri curl or used permanent relaxers, that this would make me seem more like everyone else, and no one would notice the difference in our hair.

News flash.... they noticed...no matter what I did.

In my next stage, I focused on authentic, more ethnic looking styles, braids and beads and blow outs, twists, doing anything possible to look as if I was not part of the mainstream, to show I was black and proud. However, trying so hard NOT to look like something is much more difficult than just looking like I want to look. Now, I am in a stage of contentment and happiness with who I am, the hair that God gave me, and how I look. I spend much more time now looking for hairstyles that I like, and think would look good on me, feeling comfortable being able to change it up when I am so moved.

While the microaggressions and microinsults continue about my hair, my daughter's hair, and the hair of many of my friends, by those who don't understand or who fail to understand the sanctity of the black hair experience, I am so content with the fact that I have African-Nigerian-American-kinky-straight-curly-coiled-natural-relaxed-braided-twisted-knotted-weaved-crocheted-wigged-good-bad-big-black-brown-highlighted-long-short-bobbed-layered-tough-soft-beautiful flexible, diverse hair that I am so proud of. I don't even have enough energy or interest in responding to all of the questions and statements that come from people who don't get it – I need to think of my next hairstyle and my daughter's next do!

As it's been said, if someone says to a black woman "Excuse me, but your hair is blocking my view," she should respond – "Excuse me, but my hair IS the view!"

Chapter 21

Where are You From? – The Obama Effect

"Why fit in when you were born to stand out?"
Dr. Seuss

"Where are you from?" These four words, so seemingly simple, can invoke some of the strangest and most stressful reactions from a First-Gen, depending on where in their life cycle they are.

One of the biggest struggles for the First-Gen is reconciling traditions and values of their former country or parent's former country, traditions and values of their current country and environment, and who they feel like they are internally. This is commonly seen with people of mixed race, ethnicity or ancestry because they cannot singularly identify with any one part of themselves, even though everyone wants them to fit into a box.

Along my journey, I have struggled with being a tapestry as opposed to one specific fabric. Depending on where I was in my First-Gen life cycle, I would be incredibly uncomfortable with the question – "Where are you from?" This question has always been hard to answer – sometimes because I *don't* understand the intent of the questioner – sometimes because I *do* understand the intent of the questioner – and sometimes because the answer is long and complicated. I've found myself awkwardly responding to this question with a bizarre mixture of fear, confusion, layering and doubt.

And then, we elected the 44th President of the United States, President Barack Hussein Obama, and his wife, First Lady Michelle Obama, to lead the nation and set a new tone for American politics, international relations and most important, the American identity. The image and presence of the President and First Lady not only illuminated the power of diversity in the Oval Office and inspire a new generation of children who believe that diversity is a White House standard. They validated a lot of the internal conflict that many First-Gens have. Here we were learning about our President who:

- Was the child of an African-Kenyan father and white American mother
- Was raised with his white grandparents
- Lived with his stepfather, mother and biracial sister in Indonesia
- Lived in Hawaii, Indonesia and many parts of the United States
- Transitioned from an identity with the name Barry, to one in which he reclaimed his original African name, Barack
- Pursued the highest level of education and shattered many ceilings while doing so

- Married a highly educated, African-American woman from the South Side of Chicago
- Fathered two lovely daughters; and...
- Identified with every single aspect of who he was, unabashedly, without hesitation

And this inspired what I believe was the *Obama Effect* – proudly being the sum of all your parts, and not just your parts. In the contentment phase of my first-generation life cycle, I can easily answer that awkward question with confidence, and no confusion that my tapestry makes sense. We've been validated. My intersections are a source of pride. No papaya head reasoning or insults can take this away. I am perfectly content, and depending on the scenario, I can answer that four-word question, "Where are you from?", with ease.

I'm not all Nigerian, I'm not all American. I'm not either or neither. I'm both. And I'm both at the same time. "I'm a Nigerian-American and grew up in Ohio, went to college and medical school in Ohio, trained in New York and Boston and then lived in Connecticut, where I got married and had my kids, until we moved to California." I'm complicated, wonderfully complicated.

So, last year when I was teaching my then 10-year-old son how to iron clothes and check the labels for the fabric type before setting the iron, and he asked- "Can you iron this if it's not 100% cotton or 100% polyester?" – I had the perfect response.

"Yes, you can," I said. "It's both. There's a setting for that."

Chapter 22

Parenting the Second Generation (SecGens)

I wish I could say there are no papaya heads anymore, and that we've solved that problem in America. But, being a parent of the second generation, the SecGens, makes it strikingly clear that the problems that I experienced as a First-Gen are better but not gone.

When my kids ask me to make and put Nigerian food in their lunchboxes, with the meat on the bone and everything, I constantly reflect on how different things are for them than it was for my siblings and me. I marvel when I visit my children's school at lunchtime and see children, many of them SecGens, also eating the food of their parents and grandparents. Or when I see many of the SecGens eager to go visit the countries of their parents and grandparents- Christmas in Nigeria, summer in the Philippines, Winter breaks in Vietnam, New Year in China, Easter in Ghana, January in India.

I admire the thirst of my children to learn Nigerian languages, but also to master proper English, Spanish and other languages around them, while embracing the food, cultures, humor, clothing and traditions of their many multi-cultural influences. My children enjoy celebrating Cinco de Mayo, Diwali, Carnival, Chinese/Lunar New Year, Mardi Gras, St. Patrick's Day, MLK Jr. Day, Juneteenth, and Nigerian Independence Day, going to Filipino parties and events, watching Korean K dramas, learning how to make jambalaya and Southern fried chicken. And from what I see, they are better for it.

They look forward to bi-annual trips to Nigeria and don't seem to have the insecurity that my siblings and I did about where we fit in. They are at ease answering that question "Where are you from?" and don't seem to be bothered by it like we were at their age. When they are in Nigeria and receive the kind of love and attention they get there, they feel validated. When they are in America and able to feel the power and beauty in their differences, they feel validated. When we have to have conversations about papaya head issues in the world around us, we start at a very different place. They don't feel confused about their entitlement and right to be here and thrive in America.

Chapter 23

Papaya Head – A Generation Later

A few years ago, my younger brother received a message from the daughter of the original Papaya Head, who had found a way to connect with him after over nearly decades since we had first encountered her father. As adults now, we never really thought about the impact of her father's behavior and words on *her*. Her paraphrased exchange with him went like this:

To: Emeka

Dear Emeka, I hope you remember me, and in a way, I hope you don't. My name is [First, Last] and I was your neighbor when you guys lived on [Name] Court in Columbus a long time ago. I am not even sure you were born yet, but I can't find information for your older brothers and sisters. I want to apologize to you and your whole family for my father's treatment of you guys when you lived next to us. I used to watch him assault your family and sit there in horror, unsure what to do as a little girl, but feeling I should do something. Sometimes I would say "Daddy, stop!" but he wouldn't. He spent a lot of time in my youth telling me how bad black people were and that I should never play with you guys. I would always tell him that black people I knew, including you guys, were amazing, so nice and so much fun to be with. He forbade me to talk to you guys. Although I try to erase the memories, there are some images in my head of him screaming at your Mom on the porch, with you guys standing behind her, that I cannot erase. I just can't imagine how you guys felt as children seeing that. If it was traumatic for me, I know it must have been a nightmare for you. I was secretly glad when you all moved, so I would not have to see you live through that anymore.

You all have gone on to be as amazing as I knew you would be, and although my father hasn't changed that much, I am happy that as an adult, I can actively disagree with him and I can make sure my children don't harbor that kind of hate. Please forgive me for not doing more to stop him, and if you can, forgive him too. He is not at peace with himself and he never will be until he removes that hate from his heart. I don't expect you to write me back, but I hope you accept my apology and share it with your siblings. My heart is at peace just knowing I have the opportunity to say I'm sorry.

Love,

[Name]

*P.S. There is one funny story I always remember –
one day, when my Dad was screaming at your Mom
and calling her all kinds of horrific names, your Mom
started yelling back at him with the funniest names, of
fruits and stuff. The more she did it, the more he got
upset. I kind of laughed and thought 'you go girl!' "*

We were stunned. In all of the years I had been thinking about this story, I failed to remember the little girl with dark brown hair and questioning eyes standing behind her father. I actually remember her trying to tug her father's hand and pull him inside, asking him to stop a few times. I remember her as we got to elementary school, struggling with whether she could be friends with us or not. I never knew that these same encounters were permanently etched in her memory too, and that we all had our own scars, bruises and triumphs from this situation. In a way, she and I were not that much different – we both had to figure out a way to disassemble hate in our lives. Whether it was the hate within us or the hate around us, the only way we could move forward in our lives was by making sure we intentionally got rid of it.

And, interestingly, though we heard it from two different sets of ears, we all thought "Papaya Head" and the other tropical fruit insults were funny and unique- they stuck with her just like they stuck with us. Unknowingly, our Mom drew power from things she loved to clap back. Love always wins. His daughter was right about our Mom – "You go girl."

Praise for
Papaya Head

Papaya Head is a compelling, relatable tale not only of the immigrant experience, but of the triumph of love, including self-love, over hate. A must-read for anyone who wants to understand the journey or understand that they're not alone on it.

— *Tahirah Tyrell, MD, MSc – Author, How to Take the Driver's Seat in Your Healthcare*

Dr. Olayiwola has simultaneously captured the struggle, discord and ultimate beauty of life growing up in a successful immigrant household. The poignant stories in *Papaya Head* speak to the struggle of so many—immigrants, people of color, women, first generation and multi-racial individuals—who are forming their individual identities while embracing the confluence of multiple different cultures on their lives.

— *Candy Magaña, MPA*

Excerpts from Articles about African and Other Immigrants in the United States

At an Onyejekwe family get-together, you can't throw a stone without hitting someone with a master's degree. Doctors, lawyers, engineers, professors — every family member is highly educated and professionally successful, and many have a lucrative side gig to boot. Parents and grandparents share stories of whose kid just won an academic honor, achieved an athletic title or performed in the school play. Aunts, uncles and cousins celebrate one another's job promotions or the new nonprofit one of them just started. To the Ohio-based Onyejekwes, this level of achievement is normal. They're Nigerian-American — it's just what they do.

Today, 29 percent of Nigerian-Americans over the age of 25 hold a graduate degree, compared to 11 percent of the overall U.S. population, according to the Migrations Policy Institute. Among Nigerian-American professionals, 45 percent work in education services, the 2016 American Community Survey found, and many are professors at top universities. Nigerians are entering the medical field in the U.S. at an increased rate, leaving their home country to work in American hospitals, where they can earn more and work in better facilities. A growing number of Nigerian-Americans are becoming entrepreneurs and CEOs, building tech companies in the U.S. to help people back home.

It hasn't been easy — the <u>racist stereotypes</u> are far from gone. Last year, President Donald Trump reportedly said in an Oval Office discussion that Nigerians would never go back to "their huts" once they saw America. But overt racism hasn't stopped Nigerian-Americans from creating jobs, treating patients, teaching students and contributing to local communities in their new home, all while confidently emerging as one of the country's most successful immigrant communities, with a median household income of $62,351, compared to $57,617 nationally, as of 2015.

Taken from:
The Most Successful Ethnic Group in the U.S May Surprise You
by Molly Fosco
Ozy.com
The Daily Dose
June 7, 2018

***

One of the most striking facts about immigration to the U.S., unbeknownst even to many immigration advocates, is the superior education of Africans coming to this country. If we consider adults age 25 or older, born in Africa and living in the U.S., 41.7 of them have a bachelor's degree or more, according to 2009 data. For contrast, the native-born population has a bachelor's degree or more at the much lower rate of only 28.1 percent in these estimates, and foreign-born adults as a whole have a college degree at the rate of 26.8 percent, both well below the African rate.

Taken from:
Africa Is Sending Us Its Best and Brightest
by Tyler Cowen
Bloomberg News
January 12, 2018

***

A seemingly un-American fact about America today is that for some groups, much more than others, upward mobility and the American dream are alive and well. It may be taboo to say it, but certain ethnic, religious and national-origin groups are doing strikingly better than Americans overall.

Indian-Americans earn almost double the national figure (roughly $90,000 per year in median household income versus

$50,000). Iranian-, Lebanese- and Chinese-Americans are also top-earners. In the last 30 years, Mormons have become leaders of corporate America, holding top positions in many of America's most recognizable companies. These facts don't make some groups "better" than others, and material success cannot be equated with a well-lived life. But willful blindness to facts is never a good policy.

Jewish success is the most historically fraught and the most broad-based. Although Jews make up only about 2 percent of the United States' adult population, they account for a third of the current Supreme Court; over two-thirds of Tony Award-winning lyricists and composers; and about a third of American Nobel laureates.

Taken from:
What Drives Success?
by Amy Chua and Jed Rubenfeld
New York Times Opinion
Jan. 25, 2014

***

Nigerian immigrants have the highest levels of education in this city and the nation, surpassing whites and Asians, according to Census data bolstered by an analysis of 13 annual Houston-area surveys conducted by <u>Rice University</u>.

Although they make up a tiny portion of the U.S. population, a whopping 17 percent of all Nigerians in this country held master's degrees while 4 percent had a doctorate, according to the 2006 American Community Survey conducted by the <u>U.S. Census Bureau</u>. In addition, 37 percent had bachelor's degrees.

Taken from:
Data show Nigerians the most educated in the U.S.
by Leslie Casimir
Houston Chronicle
2008

Made in the USA
San Bernardino, CA
30 October 2018